THE RIVER JORDAN

THE RIVER JORDAN

An Illustrated Guide from Bible Days to the Present

Carta, Jerusalem

A Carta Publication

Editor Barbara Ball
Map Editor Lorraine Kessel

Photographer Garo Nalbandian

Photo on page 9 Israel Antiquities Authority
Photo on page 29 Israel Government Press Office
Cover design Elizabeth Nesis

Frontispiece: Waiting to be baptized.
Title page: Detail of Madaba Map showing the River Jordan enter into the Dead Sea.

ISBN 965 220 393 9

Printed in Israel

Contents

Introduction

The river Jordan, the largest and most important of the rivers of the Holy Land, has held great historical and religious significance from earliest times. The name derives from the Hebrew word *ha-Yarden*, meaning "the [river] that descends" or "the descender." An appropriate name, for this unique river involves a drop of about 2,600 feet (800 m), from the foothills of Mount Hermon to the lowest point on earth, the Dead Sea.

The primary sources of the Jordan—Nahal Hermon (Banias), Nahal Dan and Nahal Snir (Hasbani)—with their headwaters in the foothills of Mount Hermon, converge on the way and flow into Lake Hula. The Jordan River, after passing through the Hula Basin (now being partly restored to its original marshy state) continues southward for some 10 miles (17 km) until it enters the Sea of Galilee at its northernmost point.

Emerging from the southern end of the Sea of Galilee (Israel's major reservoir of fresh water), the Jordan River changes face and meanders down to the Dead Sea, a journey of some 70 miles (117 km) as the crow flies. But the river itself, because of its extremely winding, snakelike course, actually runs almost three times this distance. As the Jordan flows downward it is fed by many lateral tributaries, the largest being

the Yarmuk River on the east. Losing most of its waters along the way, mainly through seepage and evaporation, it arrives at the Dead Sea often as a mere trickle.

The Jordan River has played an important role in the history of Israel and has provided an impressive setting for some of the most significant events mentioned in the Bible. The Jordan River is mentioned nearly 200 times in the Bible. The most important event by far is the crossing of the Jordan by the Israelites on their way to the Promised Land (Joshua 3–8:29). The men of Jabesh-gilead crossed the Jordan to recover King Saul's body from Beth-shean and return him to Jabesh for decent burial (1 Samuel 31); miracles were performed on and near the river by, among others, the prophets Elijah and Elisha; the baptism of Jesus and his sojourn in the desert took place in the area around the Jordan; and the list goes on. Small wonder that its waters are revered to the present day.

Few holy places are farther than a few miles from the river. Nazareth, for example, is less than 20 miles away, as is Jerusalem.

Within these covers we have endeavored to bring you the landscapes, towns and holy sites on both sides of the Jordan, their place in the Bible, and their significance to this day.

The River Jordan in the Bible

The Old Testament

THE CONQUEST OF THE LAND OF CANAAN

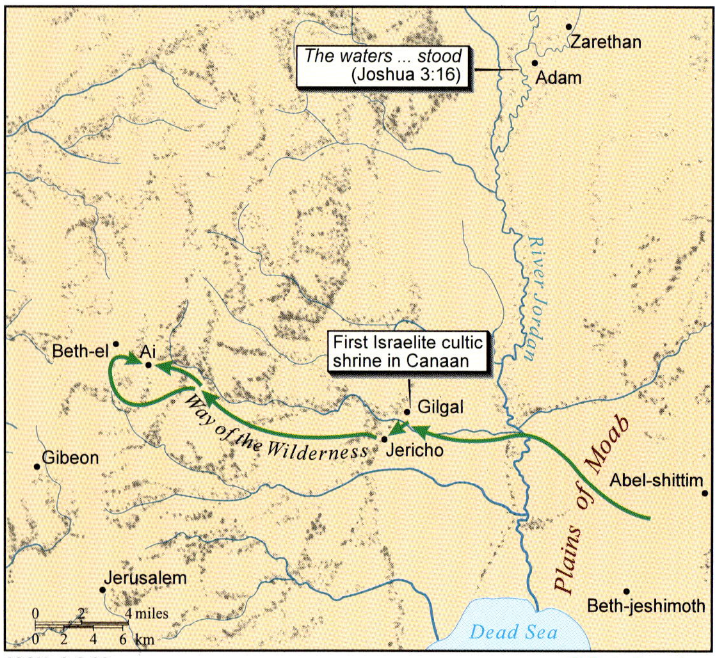

JOSH. 3-8:29

THE PURSUIT OF THE MIDIANITES ACROSS THE JORDAN

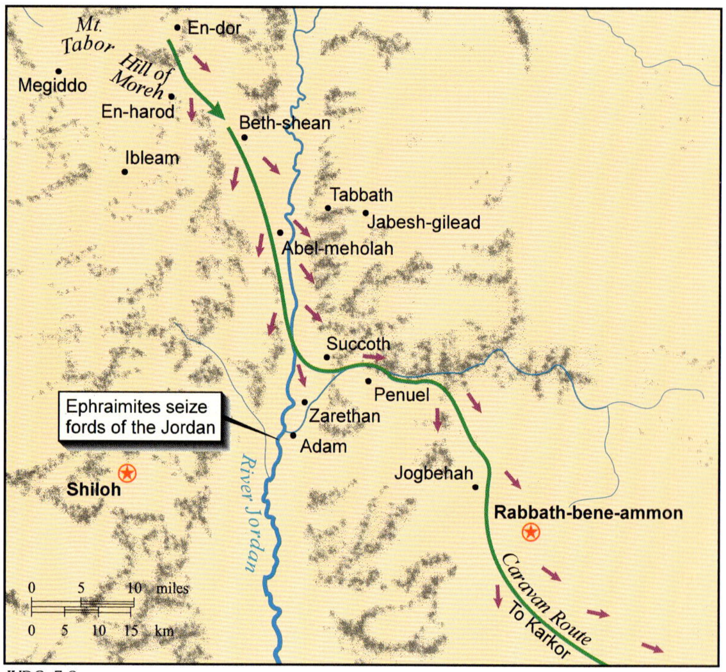

JUDG. 7-8

The River Jordan.

THE BURIAL OF SAUL

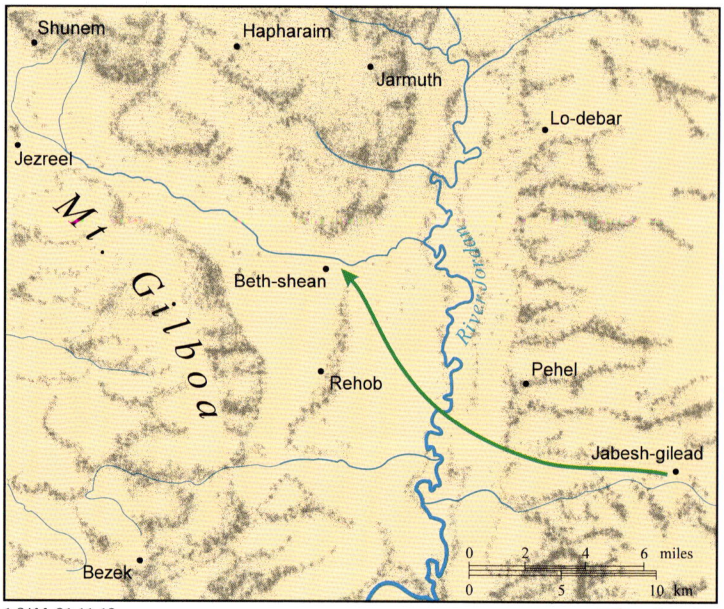

1 SAM. 31:11-13

DAVID'S FLIGHT FROM ABSALOM

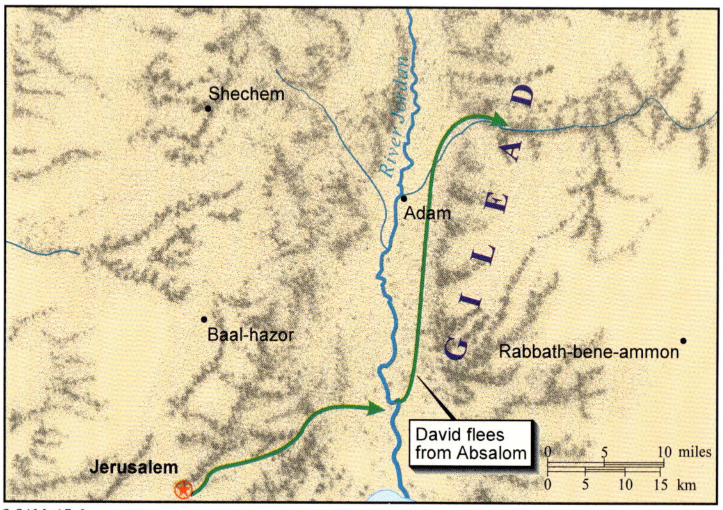

2 SAM. 15:6

The "boat of Jesus" raised from the bottom of the Sea of Galilee.

The New Testament

THE TRAVELS OF JESUS

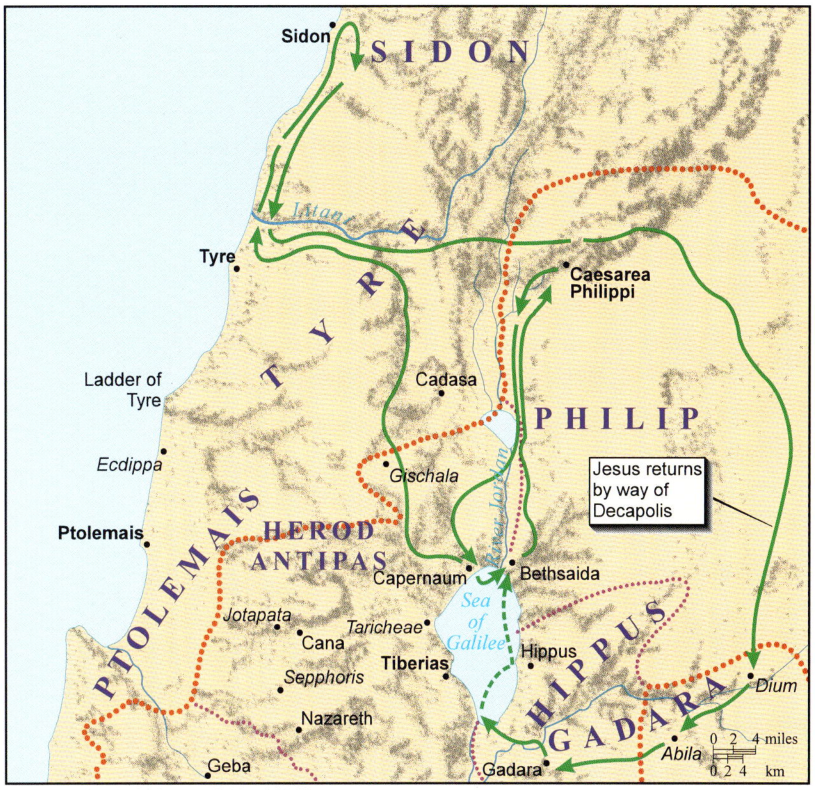

MT. 15:21-29, 16:13-20; MK. 7:24-31, 8:27-30

THE BAPTISM OF JESUS AND THE SOJOURN IN THE DESERT

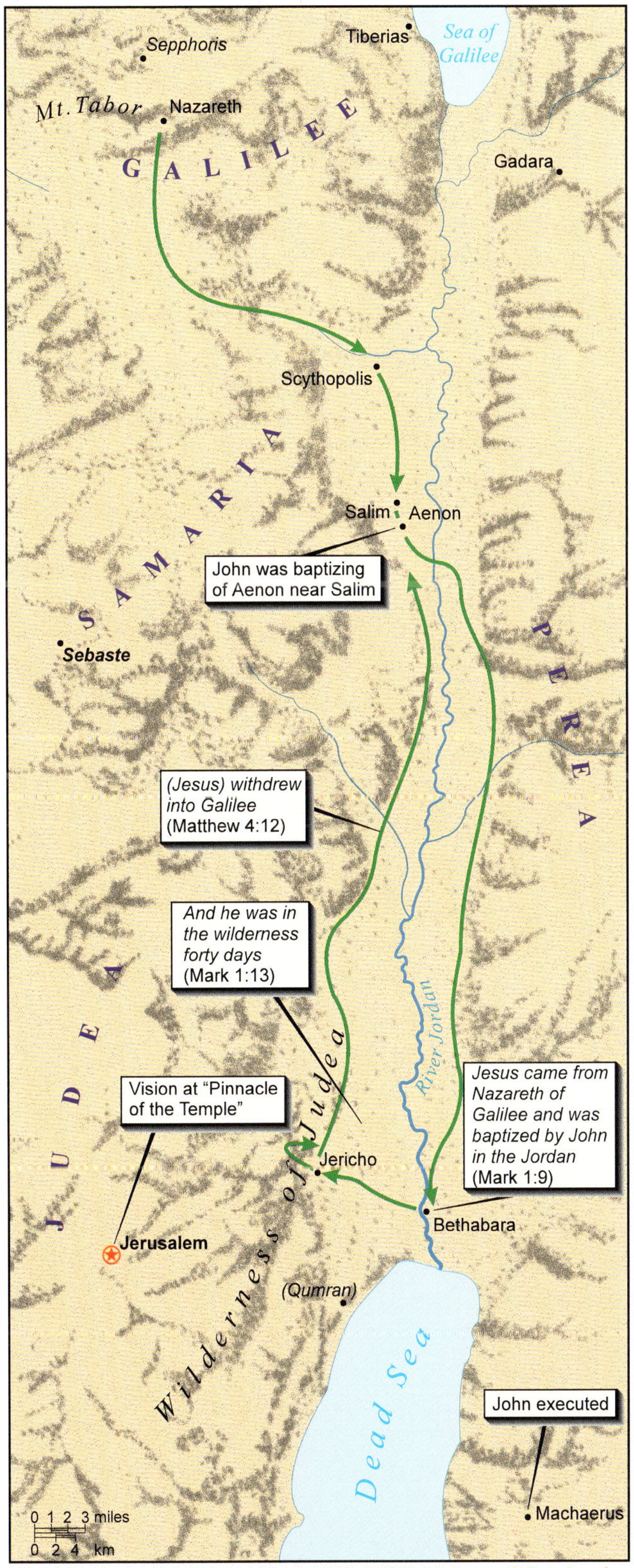

MT. 3-4:12, 14:1-2; MK. 1:4-14, 6:14-29; LK. 3:1-22, 6:18-30, 9:7-9; JN. 1:6-8, 15-42, 3:22-24

JESUS' LAST JOURNEY TO JERUSALEM

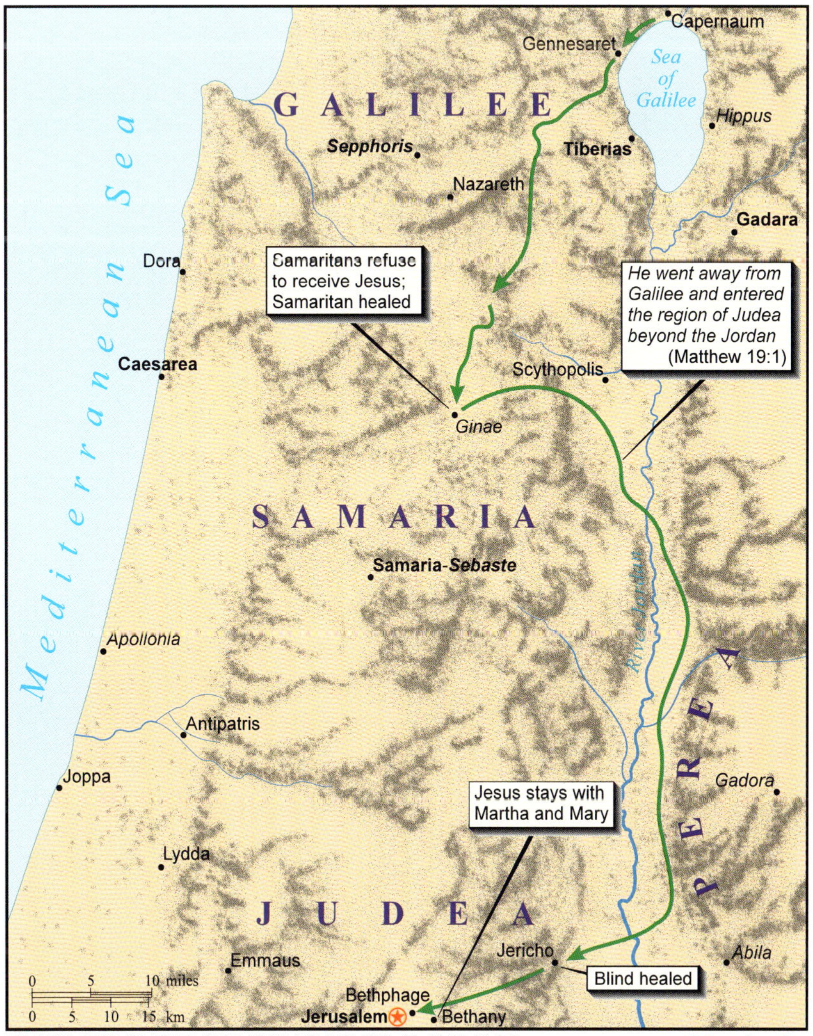

MT. 16:21, 17:22-27, 19:1-2, 20:17, 29-34; MK. 8:31, 10:1, 32, 46-52, 11:1-2; LK. 9:51-56, 10:38-42, 13:22, 18:31-42, 19:1-10, 28-35; JN. 12:1-8

From the Sources of the Jordan to the Sea of Galilee

BANIAS

Of the three sources of the Jordan, the best known is the **Banias**, a perennial stream that runs 5.5 miles (9 km) through lush woodlands and ends in a broad lagoon, with Mount Hermon as a backdrop. It is flanked by rock-hewn caves *(below)* and an ancient temple dedicated to the goat-footed Pan. Called Paneas in the Hellenistic age in honor of the Greek god, the name survives in the site's modern name, Banias (there is no "p" in the Arabic alphabet). It was here in the Roman period that Philip the Tetrarch, the son of Herod the Great, established the city of Caesarea Philippi, named thus to distinguish it from the other Caesarea, on the Mediterranean coast. At a secluded spot nearby Peter is thought to have made his famous confession to Jesus: "You are the Christ. . ." (Matthew 16:13–20, Mark 8:27–30).

DAN

Nahal Dan, another source of the Jordan River, is a perennial stream originating at **Tel Dan** *(left)*, the site of biblical Laish or Leshem. The site was renamed Dan after being conquered by the tribe of the same name. During the First Temple period, in the days of Solomon, it was the cult center of the northern tribes. It was here that Jeroboam set up one of the two golden calves (I Kings 12:28–29). The city marked the northern limit of the kingdom of Israel, as expressed in the phrase "from Dan to Beersheba" (Judges 20:1). Today the archaeological mound, the springs below and surrounding area are all part of a nature reserve.

KEDESH

Kedesh, located about 6 miles (10 km) northwest of Hazor (see below), was a Canaanite city conquered by Joshua and later given to the tribe of Naphtali. It was here that Barak and Deborah assembled the armies of Israel to fight against Sisera of the Canaanites (Judges 4:6–10). Archaeological excavations at the site not only uncovered the Canaanite city but also a Roman temple. According to the Roman historian Josephus, Titus encamped here when he set out to fight John of Gischala.

(above) Remains of a large, pillared building at Hazor, probably used as a royal storehouse, from the 9th century B.C.

(right) Remains of a Roman temple at Tel Kedesh.

HAZOR

Hazor, the largest ancient mound in the Holy Land, is some 9 miles (14 km) north of the Sea of Galilee. It is 130 feet (40 m) high, 1,970 feet (600 m) long and 660 feet (200 m) wide. Hazor was an important Canaanite city that figured prominently in the Israelite conquest of the land. The Bible relates that Jabin, king of Hazor, headed a league of Canaanite cities in the battle against Joshua at "the waters of Merom." A direct reference to the role of Hazor at the time of the Israelite conquest is found in the Book of Joshua (11:10–13): "And Joshua turned back at that time, and took Hazor, and smote its king with the sword; for Hazor formerly was the head of all those kingdoms . . . and he burned Hazor with fire." Like at Kedesh (above), Deborah and Barak fought here in their war against Sisera. In the time of Solomon, the city was fortified because of its strategic location near the waters of Merom. Excavations uncovered 22 strata of occupation, including clear evidence of Joshua's destruction. Near the mound is Kibbutz Ayelet Hashahar, with its lovely guest house, and the Hazor Museum, containing many of the finds and well worth visiting.

Around the Sea of Galilee

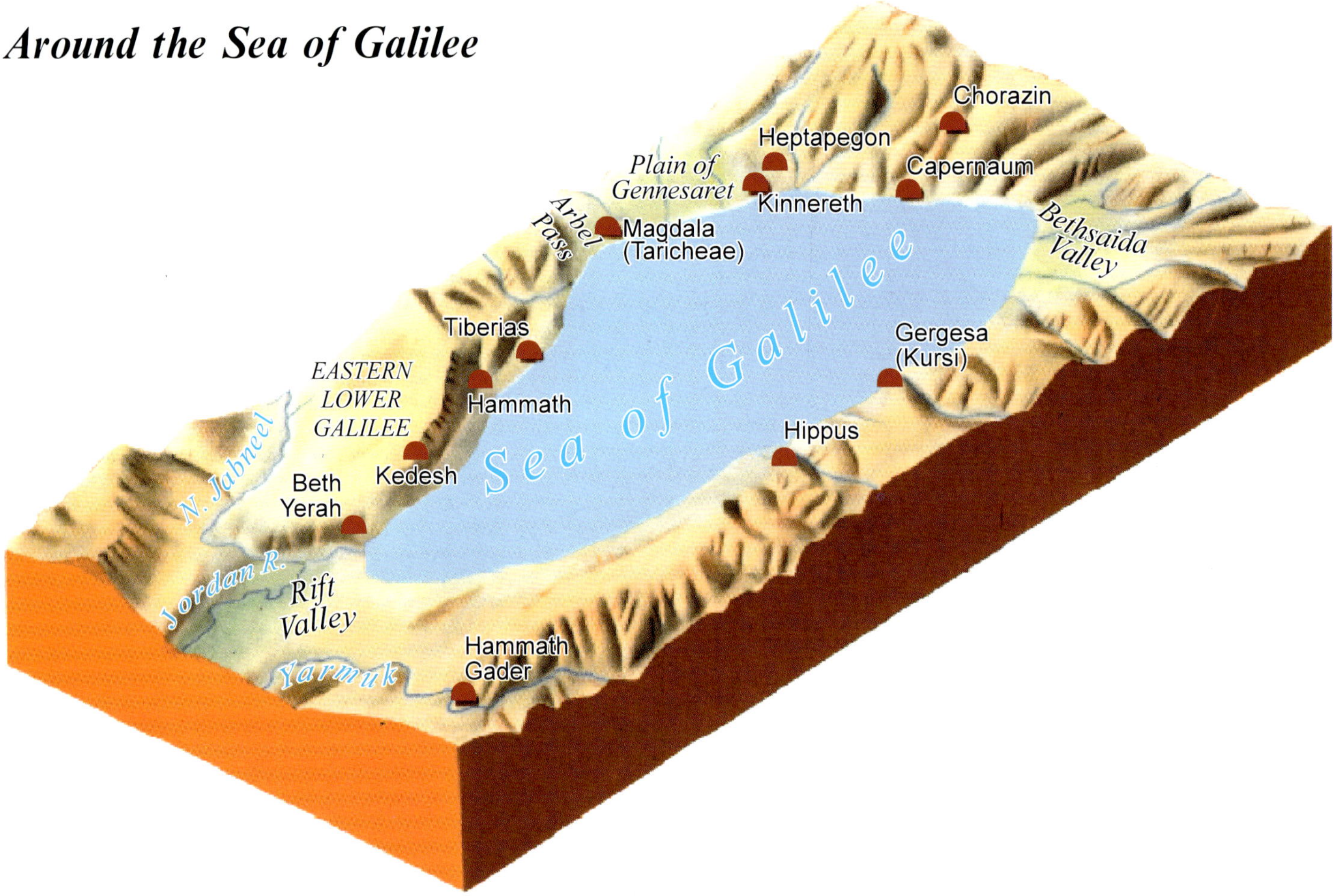

The **Sea of Galilee**, a freshwater lake in the northern Jordan Valley, is primarily associated with the miracles of Jesus. The lake is known in Hebrew as **Kinneret**, from the Hebrew word *kinnor* (harp), because of its similar shape. Other names ascribed to it are the Sea of Chinnereth, Gennesaret and the Sea of Tiberias. It is about 13 miles (21 km) long, 7.5 miles (12 km) wide, and 130 to 160 feet (40 – 50 m) deep, depending on the amount of winter rainfall and snow melting from Mount Hermon. Its narrow shores are surrounded by three fertile valleys: **Ginnesar** (Gennesaret) on the northwest, **Bethsaida** *(below)*, the scene of the feeding of the five thousand (Luke 9:10), on the northeast, and the **Jordan Valley** to the south. The lake and many adjacent sites are holy to Christians. Much of Jesus' public ministry took place at sites along its northern shores and it was here that Jesus walked on water.

(above) The Sea of Galilee and its environs, looking east. (below) Remains of the 3rd–4th century basalt synagogue at Chorazin.

CHORAZIN

Chorazin, northwest of the Sea of Galilee, was a Jewish town in the Roman-Byzantine period. It is mentioned in the Books of Matthew (11:21) and Luke (10:13) as one of the three cities, together with **Bethsaida** and **Capernaum**, that Jesus cursed because their inhabitants failed to accept his teachings. Archaeological excavations have uncovered a black basalt synagogue from the third to fourth centuries, similar to that of Capernaum, with carved decorations, Jewish symbols and inscriptions in Aramaic and Hebrew. Erected in the form of a basilica, the most interesting feature is the "Seat of Moses," a single block of basalt carved in the shape of a chair where the teacher may have sat while reading the Law.

The "Seat of Moses" at Chorazin.

The 3rd-century synagogue at Capernaum.

CAPERNAUM

Capernaum, on the northwestern shore of the Sea of Galilee, was the center of Jesus' Galilean ministry. Capernaum was located along the ancient highway leading to the kingdoms of the Fertile Crescent. Its Hebrew name, **Kefar Nahum**, is traditionally named after the prophet Nahum. It was well known during the Second Temple, Roman and Byzantine periods. It is important as the birthplace of Peter, and this is where Jesus once lived, preached and performed miracles. In the fourth century a Jewish apostate, Joseph of Tiberias, built a church here and in time the place became a pilgrimage center. Although the site was apparently destroyed in the sixth century, it seems to have been resettled and even flourished until the tenth century.

The most significant find is a third century synagogue built over an earlier one, possibly that in which Jesus preached. The typically early Byzantine synagogue was reconstructed in 1921 by the Franciscans. The gallery is adorned by stone friezes depicting a menorah, vine leaves, bunches of grapes, dates, hexagram, pentagram, shofar, a Torah ark and tabernacle. A Greek and Aramaic inscription was found on two column fragments. There is also a Greek Orthodox church and monastery on the shores of the Sea of Galilee, on the site of a Byzantine church dedicated to St. John the Theologian.

TABGHA (HEPTAPEGON)

Tabgha (Heptapegon) is located on the northwestern shore of the Sea of Galilee, a short distance south of Capernaum. The modern name of the site, Tabgha, is a distortion of the Greek name Heptapegon, meaning the "place of seven springs." Of the seven springs that flowed into the Sea of Galilee, only five survive today. The **Church of the Multiplication of the Loaves and Fishes**, built here to commemorate the miracle performed by Jesus, was built on the ruins of a fourth century church. A beautiful fifth century mosaic floor, depicting a lake with fowl and flora, has been preserved from the ancient church. Another church, on the lakeshore itself, commemorates the Apparition of the Risen Christ to the Apostles and is also known as the **Church of the Primacy**, in honor of St. Peter to whom Jesus gave primacy over the other disciples.

MOUNT OF BEATITUDES

The Mount of Beatitudes is the traditional site where Jesus gave his Sermon on the Mount. The name of the mount derives from the opening words of the sermon, "Blessed are." The mount is located just behind Capernaum, 410 feet (125 m) above the lake. A monastery and church were built at the foot of the mount in the fourth century but were destroyed in the seventh century during the Arab conquest of the land. The modern octagonal church on the summit, built in 1937 by the Franciscans, gives a superb view of the lake below.

(below left) The Church of the Multiplication at Tabgha.

(below right and bottom) The Church of Beatitudes.

(opposite) The remains at Magdala.

MAGDALA

Staying on the western side of the lake, one reaches ancient "Magadan" ("Dalmanutha," in Mark 8:10), more correctly known as **Magdala**, the site of ancient **Migdal**; other names ascribed to it are Magdala Nunaya (*nun* means fish in Aramaic), Magdala Taricheae (Greek, "Magdala of the fish salters") and Magdala Tzaba'aya (Aramaic, "Magdala of the dyers"). The town was famous for its fish-curing industry and was the traditional birthplace and home of Mary Magdalene, who followed Jesus to Jerusalem. She was one of a group of women "who had been healed of evil spirits and infirmities . . . from whom seven demons had gone out" (Luke 8:2). The Roman historian Josephus describes a town of importance and even made this his headquarters during the Jewish Revolt against Rome (A.D. 70). Excavations at the site have uncovered parts of paved roads, remains of a villa with a swimming pool, a public building, water system, and a first century structure thought to be a synagogue.

THE ANCIENT BOAT

On the lakeshore nearby is **Ginnosar**, a kibbutz which houses a first century boat that was discovered in the Sea of Galilee in January 1986. The boat is about 27 feet (8.2 m) long, 7.5 feet (2.3 m) wide, and 4 feet (1.2 m) deep at the stern. Study of the workmanship shows that the boat was apparently built by a master craftsman. Based on pottery found in conjunction with the boat, construction techniques, and carbon-14 dating, the boat can be dated approximately between 100 B.C. and A.D. 70. According to Josephus, the Gospels, and a first century mosaic depiction of a boat found at Migdal, it appears that a type of large-size craft did exist on the Sea of Galilee in the first century. This type of boat usually had a crew of five and could carry as many as 15 persons in all. This extraordinary find, sometimes dubbed the "Boat of Jesus," is at present submerged in a specially built conservation pool at the kibbutz, open to the public.

TIBERIAS

Tiberias *(above)* lies on the western shore of the Sea of Galilee, about 12 miles (19 km) southwest of the entrance of the Jordan River into the lake and about 6 miles (10 km) north of the river's exit in the south. It was founded between A.D. 18 and 20 by Herod's son Herod Antipas, who made it the capital of his kingdom, and was named after the emperor Tiberius. According to the Roman historian Josephus, Tiberias was located "in the best region of Galilee." The king attracted residents to the city "by equipping houses at his own expense and adding new gifts of land" (*Antiquities* 18.36–38). A magnificent royal palace was built here, as were royal treasure houses, archives, and a huge synagogue capable of accommodating a large crowd. It maintained its status as the capital of Galilee until it was annexed in A.D. 61 to the kingdom of Agrippa II, whose capital was at Caesarea Philippi (Banias; see above). Tiberias became an important Jewish center of rabbinic learning, and by the second century it was considered, along with Jerusalem, Hebron and Safed, one of the four sacred cities of the Holy Land. The town later expanded southward until it joined with the adjacent city of **Hammath**, famous for its hot springs and medicinal baths, remains of which are still visible. The city today is a popular holiday resort with hotels and restaurants along the lakeside.

HIPPUS

Traveling around to the eastern side of the lake, one reaches **Hippus (Susita)**, located about a mile east of the Sea of Galilee on a promontory approximately 1,150 feet (350 m) in height. Hippus was founded by the Seleucids in the Hellenistic period (332–37 B.C.), possibly on the site of an earlier settlement. The town, known by its Greek name Antiochia Hippus (*hippus*, "horse"), continued to exist until the Arab conquest, in about 636. Alexander Jannaeus conquered and annexed this area to the Hasmonean kingdom. Pompey made Susita a gentile city and one of the ten Decapolis cities. The incident of the "Gadarene swine" is thought by some to have occurred within the territory of Hippus. During the Byzantine period, Hippus was the seat of a bishop and, like many other towns of the period, enjoyed great prosperity. Excavations have uncovered the remains of four churches, one of which was probably a cathedral, a city wall, a theater, columns *(opposite, below)* and two aqueducts that carried water for a distance of 15.5 miles (25 km).

GERGESA (KURSI)

Gergesa (Kursi, *above*) is situated on the eastern shore of the Sea of Galilee, some 3 miles (5 km) north of En Gev. Tradition has it that this was the site where Jesus healed two demoniacs by permitting the demons that had possessed them to enter a herd of swine, which then rushed down a steep slope into the Sea of Galilee (Matthew 8:28–34). The same incident is described in Mark and Luke. The town itself is not mentioned—only the adjective, which varies between the country of the Gadarenes, referring to the nearest city (Gadara; see p.44); of the Gerasenes, from the most important city of the district (see Jerash, p.45); or, in this case, of the Gergesenes, a purely local name. After excavations uncovering the remains of a Byzantine monastery and church had been completed at the site, remains of a square tower and a small chapel were found on the slope southeast of the monastery. The location of these remains, only about 218 yards (200 m) southeast of the church, supports the identification of the site with the locale of the miracle of the Gadarene swine because the topographical conditions are so similar to those described in the Gospel account.

HAMMATH GADER

Hammath Gader (in Arabic, **El Hammeh**) lies in the bed of the Yarmuk River, 4.5 miles (7 km) east of the Sea of Galilee. The site is named after the ancient city of **Gadara**. The hot springs and baths here have been renowned for their medicinal properties since antiquity. The baths were described by a Greek biographer at the end of the fourth century as second in beauty only to those of Baia in the Bay of Naples. The remains of the bath complex *(below)*, a Roman theater and a sixth century synagogue with mosaic floor were uncovered. The site, now renovated, is open to the public and includes baths, services and pleasant gardens.

Galilee

Galilee is a hilly region in the northern part of Israel. It is bounded on the north by the Litani River, in Lebanon, on the east by the Jordan Valley, on the south by the Jezreel (Esdraelon) Valley, and on the west by the northern coastal plain (also known as the Galilee coast). It is the land of the New Testament, where Jesus grew to manhood and performed his first miracles. Jesus devoted most of his earthly ministry to Galilee and became known as "the Galilean" (Matthew 26:69).

NAZARETH

Nazareth, located in the lower Galilee about halfway between the Sea of Galilee and the Mediterranean Sea, was the hometown of Jesus' parents, Mary and Joseph, and the place where the angel went to announce his coming birth. After Jesus' birth in Bethlehem and the flight into Egypt to escape the treachery of Herod the Great, Mary and Joseph returned with Jesus to Nazareth, where Jesus grew to manhood. Landlocked Nazareth was less conducive to the new teachings of Jesus than was Capernaum, which had a more diverse population and was closer to the borders of the Decapolis. Jesus was rejected by his townspeople and cast out of the synagogue at Nazareth (Luke 4:16–30). Yet he never entirely severed his ties with the town of his youth. He returned later in his ministry only to be rejected again (Matthew 13:53–58). Nazareth, today a city of about 40,000, is dominated by the majestic **Basilica of the Annunciation**, built on the traditional spot where the angel Gabriel announced to Mary that she would give birth to a son. The basilica is a blend of modern architectural styles and preserves a medieval structure. It is decorated with works of art from around the world. About a mile north of the basilica is the Greek Orthodox **Church of St. Gabriel**, and adjacent to it **Mary's Well**, where the angel appeared before the Virgin. Close by, east of St. Joseph's Church, is the Greek Orthodox **Synagogue Church**, believed to be on the site of the synagogue where Jesus preached.

CANA IN GALILEE

Some 4 miles (6 km) northeast of Nazareth, on the road to Tiberias, is the Arab village of Kafr Kana, identified with Cana in Galilee. This is where Jesus had performed his first miracle, turning water into wine during a wedding feast (John 2:1–11). It was here too (John 4:46) that Jesus told to a nobleman from Capernaum of the healing of his apparently dying son. Cana was also the home of Nathanael, one of Jesus' disciples (John 21:2). Today Kafr Kana is a village of about 12,000 people, mostly Muslims, the rest Christians. The Franciscans built a church here called the Church of the Miracle, which contains a replica of a jar used by Jesus. Near the Latin church is a Greek Orthodox church commemorating the same miracle, and it contains two jars, also supposedly used by Jesus.

(above) Panoramic view of Nazareth.
(left) The Franciscan and Greek churches at Cana.

SEPPHORIS

Sepphoris, about 2.5 miles (4 km) northwest of Nazareth, was the capital of Galilee in the time of Jesus. Although Sepphoris is not mentioned in the Bible, Jesus probably knew it well. Tradition has it that this was the birthplace and home of the Virgin Mary's mother, Anne. The site is first mentioned by Josephus in connection with the reign of Alexander Jannaeus and the war he fought nearby. After King Herod's death, the Romans conquered the city and sold its inhabitants into slavery. Sepphoris was rebuilt by Herod's son, Herod Antipas, who resided there and made it his capital until he founded Tiberias (see above) as the new capital of Galilee. Ancient Sepphoris is identified with the ruined village of Safuriyye, the present-day moshav Tzipori. The main finds uncovered here so far date to the Roman and Byzantine periods. Ruins of a Crusader fortress, built on top of earlier Roman foundations, were found at the summit of the site. Other remains include a Roman theater, a palatial mansion, and a number of magnificent buildings adorned with colorful mosaic floors, some of exceptional workmanship. One in particular, a large Byzantine structure, has in its largest room a figurative mosaic depicting the Nile festival and various hunting scenes.

(right) Crusader fortress at Sepphoris.
(below) Mount Tabor.
(bottom) The village of Nein, site of biblical Nain.

MOUNT TABOR

Mount Tabor is a dome-shaped mountain in Galilee in the heart of the Jezreel Valley. Mentioned several times in the Old Testament, Christians know it for the Gospel story of the Transfiguration of Christ (Matthew 17:1–3), which tradition places on Mount Tabor. Today a Franciscan church stands here—the Basilica of the Transfiguration, which commemorates the miraculous event. It was built in 1921 on the ruins of a fourth century basilica. A mosaic of the Transfiguration decorates the apse. Alongside the church are remains of Roman fortifications, wall fragments, a Crusader tower and a Franciscan monastery with a Crusader gate. Nearby is the Greek Orthodox Church of Elias (Elijah).

NAIN

Nain, identified with the modern Arab village of Nein, is a short distance from Mount Tabor, at the foot of the **Hill of Moreh** (Giv'at Hamoreh), near where the Midianites were camped when Gideon attacked them (Judges 7:1), about 3 miles (5 km) northeast of modern Afula. Jesus performed the miracle of reviving the dead youth at Nain (Luke 7:11–17). A Franciscan church commemorating the event is built here over the ruins of a Crusader church.

(top) The colonnaded street and (above) the Roman theater at Tel Beth Shean.

BETH SHEAN (SCYTHOPOLIS)

Continuing southeast toward the Jordan Valley, one reaches ancient **Beth Shean (Scythopolis)**, one of the oldest, almost continuously occupied sites in the country. The reason for its long survival lies in its highly strategic location at the junction of two important routes: the road leading east to west from the Jezreel and Harod valleys to Gilead in Jordan, and the road running the length of the Jordan Valley from north to south. During the Israelite conquest, Beth-shean was allotted to the tribe of Manasseh but continued to be occupied by the Canaanites. After King Saul and his sons died on Mount Gilboa, the Philistines fastened their bodies to the wall of Beth-shean, where a temple to Ashtaroth was located. The men of Jabesh-gilead valiantly rescued the bodies and buried them in Jabesh (1 Samuel 31:8–12). David later recovered the remains and gave them a proper burial in the land of Benjamin (2 Samuel 21:12–14). In New Testament times Beth-shean was known as Scythopolis and was one of the largest cities of the Decapolis. Excavations have revealed rich finds, dating from as early as the Neolithic period (c. 5000 B.C.) up through the early Arab period (seventh century A.D.). The Roman theater here is the best preserved in the country. Other significant finds include remains of Egyptian temples and palaces from the Late Bronze Age; remains of magnificent buildings from Roman and later periods; a Roman villa; the "House of Leontius," a basilica-like synagogue from the fourth or fifth century; a colonnaded street; an ornamental pool; and much more.

Samaria

The hill country of Samaria is where monotheism was first established. Abraham erected the first altar to God near Shechem (Nablus). After the division of Solomon's kingdom, Samaria became the center of the Northern Kingdom of Israel, from the tenth through eighth centuries B.C. In 887 B.C. the city of Samaria became the capital of the kingdom and persisted until its destruction in 721 by Sargon, king of Assyria, who deported large numbers of its population. Those who remained mixed with the foreign settlers whom the Assyrians had brought from other lands. They eventually developed a separate national entity—the **Samaritans**. They accepted the Pentateuch and the Book of Joshua, but no other part of the Bible, and to this day regard Mount Gerizim as their holy shrine. In the time of Jesus, the relationship between the Jews and the Samaritans was so strained that Jews traveling between Judea and Galilee would bypass Samaria, going instead through the barren land of Perea on the eastern side of the Jordan. Jesus, however,

(above) The hills of Gilboa.

(far left) Remains of a Samaritan temple on the top of Mount Gerizim.

(above right) Samaritan elders before a ceremony on Mount Gerizim.

rebuked his disciples for their hostility to the Samaritans (Luke 9:55 – 56), healed a Samaritan leper and praised him for his gratitude (ibid. 17:11 – 18), and asked for a drink from a Samaritan woman (John 4:7). To this day there is a small Samaritan community near Nablus.

MOUNT GILBOA

Mount Gilboa is a range of hills running southeast to northwest between the Jezreel and Beth Shean valleys. Its highest peak is about 1,760 feet (536 m) above sea level. It has little rainfall and sparse vegetation. Mount Gilboa is mentioned several times in the Bible. It was included within the tribal allotments of Issachar and Manasseh. The battles of Deborah and Gideon were fought in this region. King Saul had gathered his forces here to do battle against the Philistines, and it was at Mount Gilboa that he and his three sons were slain (1 Samuel 31:8).

SAMARIA (SEBASTE)

The ruins of the ancient city of Samaria (in Roman times called Sebaste) are located about 5 miles (8 km) northwest of Shechem. The city was built by Omri, the king of Israel, at the end of the ninth century B.C. It was the capital of the Northern Kingdom of Israel until it was destroyed by the Assyrian king Sargon in 721 B.C., when its inhabitants were deported and replaced by foreigners brought by the Assyrians. The city became the capital of an Assyrian province and later the capital of Babylonian and Persian provinces, as well. It became a Hellenistic center until destroyed by John Hyrcanus, the Hasmonean. It was rebuilt by Alexander Jannaeus, and the building continued during the Roman period. Emperor Augustus presented the city to Herod the Great, who then turned it into a magnificent Roman city, calling it Sebaste in honor of the emperor (Sebastos, meaning magnificent, was the Greek name for Augustus). Excavations here have revealed remains of walls, royal palaces, houses and storerooms from the time of the kings of Israel; the oldest standing Hellenistic tower; and remains of a splendid Herodian palace, hippodrome, theater, colonnaded street with shops, and temple. According to one tradition, John the Baptist is buried here. His tomb is found inside a Crusader church, built on the ruins of a Byzantine structure and converted into a mosque by Arabs.

SHECHEM (NABLUS)

Nablus (Shechem) is an Arab city in the Samarian Hills between **Mount Gerizim** and **Mount Ebal**. At its eastern outskirts is Tell Balata, the site of biblical Shechem. It is mentioned as the first place in Canaan associated with Abram's arrival in the land. After being promised the land to his descendants, Abram responded by building an altar to the Lord (Genesis 12:6–7). Jacob also erected an altar here (ibid. 33:18–19). Dinah, the daughter of Jacob, was raped here and avenged by her brothers Simeon and Levi, who destroyed the city (ibid. 34). During the Israelite conquest the border between Ephraim and Manasseh passed through Shechem (Joshua 17:7). It was one of the six cities of refuge (ibid. 20:7). The bones of Joseph, brought up from Egypt, were buried here (ibid. 24:32). After the division of the United Kingdom of Israel, Shechem became the residence of Jeroboam, who made it the capital of his kingdom (1 Kings 12:25). After the destruction of the kingdom of Israel, the king of Assyria replaced the city's residents with exiled Cuthians, who in time became the Samaritans and made Shechem their political and religious center. Alexander the Great permitted a Samaritan temple to be built on Mount Gerizim. In 129 B.C. John Hyrcanus seized Shechem and destroyed the temple. Following the Jewish Revolt against Rome, the emperor Titus rebuilt the city in A.D. 72 and renamed it Flavia Neapolis (whence the

Arabic name, Nablus), built on the northern slope of Mount Gerizim. In the New Testament, Jesus visited the Samaritan woman at Sychar (sometimes identified with Shechem), the site of **Jacob's Well** (John 4:5), which today is found in the Arab village of Askar, just east of Nablus.

(opposite page) A colonnaded street in Samaria (Sebaste).

(right) Church built over Jacob's Well.

(below) The ruins of Shiloh.

(bottom) Modern Nablus.

SHILOH

Continuing about 12 miles (20 km) south on the Shechem–Ramallah road, the Canaanite city of Shiloh is reached. It was a religious center after the Israelite conquest, becoming the home of Israel's tabernacle (Joshua 18:1). The Benjaminites seized the daughters of Shiloh for wives as they came out to dance (Judges 21:19–23). It was apparently destroyed by the Philistines after their victory over the Israelites at Ebenezer (Jeremiah 26:6). Excavations here uncovered remains of the Canaanite city and later towns (including two Byzantine church floors).

Judea

Judea, formerly called Judah, is a hilly region that was at the heart of the Kingdom of Judah. Its capital, Jerusalem, is holy to Jews, Christians and Muslims alike. The region is bounded by Samaria on the north, the Shephelah on the west, the Negev on the south, and the Dead Sea on the east. The area was first named Judea following the Babylonian exile. Herod the Great had the title "king of Judea" and this was the setting for most of his ambitious building projects. Elijah, Jesus, and the early monks all roamed this wilderness.

AI

Ai, identified with et-Tell, is about 3 miles (5 km) east of Ramallah. Ai figures most prominently in the account of the conquest of the land; it was the second city to fall after Jericho to the Israelites (Joshua 7–8). The ark of the covenant was kept here in the time of the Judges. Excavations here uncovered city remains from about 3310 to 2400 B.C., at which time it was destroyed and abandoned. A new, unwalled town was built in the acropolis area of the ancient ruin in about 1220 B.C. It was occupied until about 1050 B.C. and never resettled.

GIBEON

Gibeon, the modern el-Jib, was a city of Benjamin northwest of Jerusalem. It was here that Joshua called on the sun to stand still to give him time for more fighting (Joshua 10:12). The men of David and Saul fought their battle by the pool at Gibeon (2 Samuel 2:13ff). The site was an important cult center before the Temple at Jerusalem was built. The Gibeonites participated in the building of Jerusalem's walls in the time of Nehemiah. Excavations here uncovered remains of buildings, a winery, a rock-cut pool some 80 feet (25 m) deep with a spiral staircase (mentioned in 2 Samuel 2:12–17; Jeremiah 41:12), tombs and pottery from the Middle and Late Bronze (Canaanite) ages and a massive city wall from the Israelite period. A Crusader church was also found here.

The village of Qubeiba, popularly identified with Emmaus.

opposite page:
(above) A general view of Tel Ai.
(below) The pool of Gibeon.

EMMAUS

Emmaus is, according to Luke (24:13), the village where Jesus appeared to two of his disciples, after his resurrection. The actual location is disputed, but the one site which has received the most support is **Qubeiba**, an Arab village in the Judean Hills just west of **el-Jib (Gibeon)** and about 7.5 miles (12 km) northwest of **Jerusalem**. Here are remains of a Crusader fortress and church, built over ruins of a Byzantine church that was in turn erected over ruins of an ancient room, believed to be the house of Cleopas who had seen the risen Christ in Emmaus. What remains of the traditional house of Cleopas is enclosed in glass.

BETHLEHEM

Bethlehem, a town about 4 miles (7 km) south of Jerusalem, is the birthplace of Jesus Christ and thus holy to Christians the world over. In Jacob's time it was known as Ephrath and was the burial place of the matriarch Rachel (Genesis 35:19). It is the scene of the story of Ruth and the place where David was born and anointed king (1 Samuel 16:13). Bethlehem today has many Christian churches, monasteries and other religious institutes. The most renowned is the **Church of the Nativity**, built over the cave where Jesus is believed to have been born. The church was first built in the days of Constantine in 330, destroyed in the sixth century, and rebuilt in the days of Justinian. It is a fortress-like structure, divided into sections: the central part is held by the Greek Orthodox, the southern section by Armenians, and the northern part is divided between Catholics and Protestants. Today's basilica dates from the sixth century with extensive repairs from the Crusader period. The adjoining Latin Church of St. Catherine to the west is the site of midnight mass every Christmas eve. On the southeastern outskirts of Bethlehem is the traditional site of **Shepherds' Field**, where the shepherds heard the voices of the angels bidding them to hasten to Bethlehem to adore the Child. To this day shepherds roam with their flocks in the open fields around Bethlehem.

(opposite page) Bethlehem, with the Moab Mountains in the background.

(right) Plan of the Church of the Nativity in Bethlehem.

(below) Shepherds' Field near Bethlehem.

(overleaf) Bethlehem (above) and Jerusalem (below).

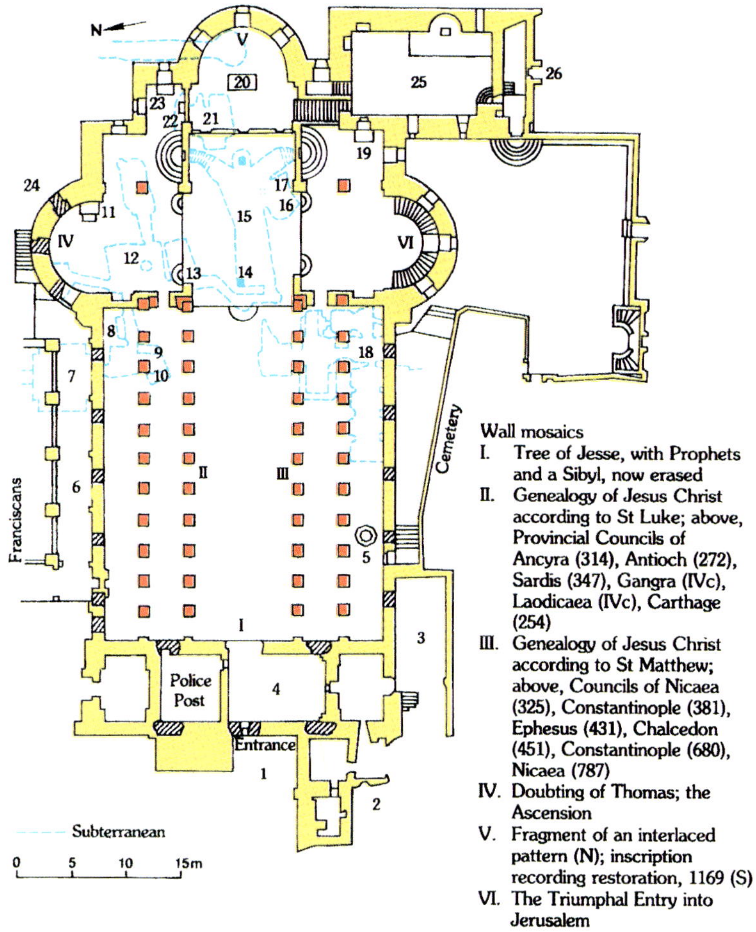

1. Courtyard; 2. Armenian monastery; 3. Armenian courtyard; 4. Narthex; 5. Font; 6. Cloister; 7. Chapel of St Jerome; 8. Altar of St Eusebius; 9. Sts Paula and Eustochium; 10. St Jerome; 11. Altar of the Virgin; 12. Tombs of the Holy Innocents; 13. Altar of St Joseph; 14. Cistern; 15. Grotto of the Nativity; 16. Manger; 17. Altar of the Magi; 18. Burial grottoes; 19. Altar of the Circumcision; 20. Main altar; 21. Cistern; 22. Star of the Nativity; 23. Altar of Kings; 24. Church of St Catherine; 25. Sacristy and Chapel of St George; 26. Bell tower

JERUSALEM

Jerusalem is sacred to the world's three great monotheistic religions—Judaism, Christianity, and Islam. It was a Jebusite city captured by King David in about 1000 B.C. Both David and his son Solomon made it capital of their kingdoms. The First Temple, built in the days of Solomon, was destroyed by the Babylonians in 586 B.C. A little more than five centuries later, under the rule of the Herodian dynasty and the Roman governors (67 B.C.–A.D. 70), Jerusalem reached the pinnacle of its prosperity and beauty. Herod the Great had a passion for embellishment, expressed in the magnitude and style of his building projects. (A scale model of Jerusalem in the Herodian period is on view next to the Holyland Hotel, in the southwestern part of the new city.) Herod built palaces, erected fortifications, and renovated the Temple on Mount Moriah (the Temple Mount), all with a magnificence previously unknown in Jerusalem. This was the Jerusalem that Jesus had known. According to the Gospel of Luke, Jesus went with his parents to Jerusalem when he was twelve years old. He stayed behind in the Holy City, where he was found debating with the teachers in the Temple. The Gospel according to John records several more of Jesus' journeys to Jerusalem. Jesus spent his last days in the Holy City and it was here that his trial, judgment, crucifixion, resurrection and ascension took place. Archaeological discoveries and literary sources, namely, the Gospels and the descriptions of Josephus, provide the basis for reconstructing the city in Jesus' time and locating the holy sites, many of which have been venerated for centuries by the erection of churches and other structures.

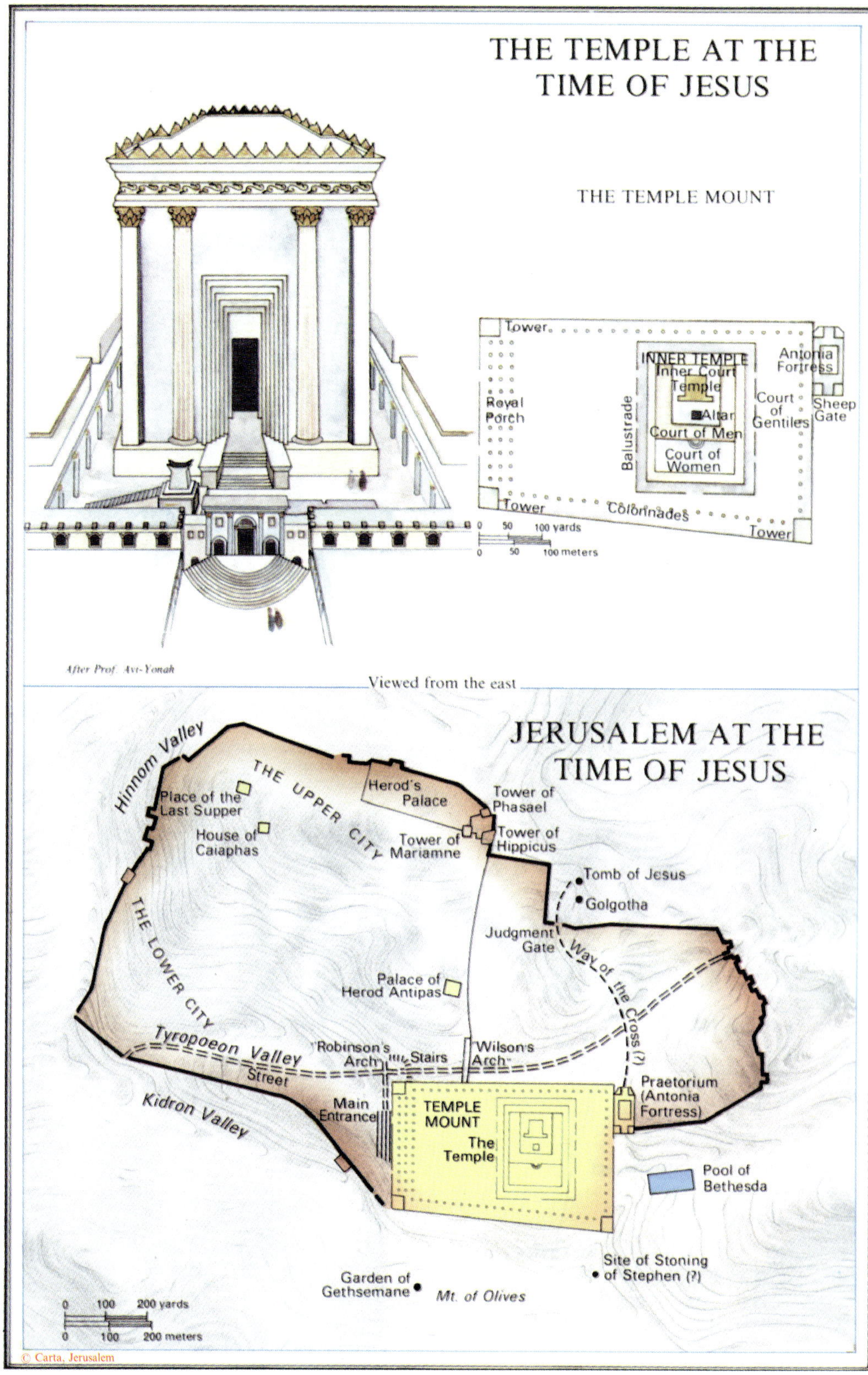

(opposite, above) The Dome of the Ascension in Jerusalem.

(opposite, below) The Church of Lazarus in Bethany.

BETHANY

Bethany is the site where Jesus resurrected Lazarus, the brother of Mary and Martha (John 11), and attended the feast at Simon's house (Matthew 26). Bethany is identified with modern el-Eizariya, an Arab village at the eastern approach to Jerusalem. The grotto on the traditional site of Lazarus' tomb was enshrined in the fourth century; it has 27 steps leading down to the tomb. In the sixteenth century Muslims built a mosque over the grotto and in the following century Christians were allowed to pray inside. Today, the Franciscan Church of Lazarus, built in 1952, stands over the grotto.

Judean Wilderness

The Judean Wilderness (*above*) is a hilly desert region about 60 miles (100 km) long and 12.5 miles (20 km) wide, sandwiched between the Judean Hills and the Jordan Valley.

DEIR EL QURUNTUL

The baptism of Jesus, which took place either at Bethabara, at the fords of the Jordan near Jericho (modern **Qasr el Yahud**), or higher up the river at Aenon, south of **Scythopolis (Beth Shean)**, was followed by forty days of seclusion in the wilderness of Judea. To commemorate this event, a Greek Orthodox monastery, about 2.5 miles (4 km) northwest of Jericho, was built into the side of a sheer cliff overlooking the Jericho oasis *(opposite)*. Its Arabic name, **Deir el Quruntul**, derives from the Latin word *quarantena*, meaning forty days. Tradition has it that Jesus spent the forty days of temptation in a cave near here. The original monks who moved here early in the fourth century lived in the natural caves in the cliff. Later a monastery was built but destroyed by the Persians. The present structure was contructed between 1875 and 1905.

JERICHO

Jericho, in the southern Jordan Valley, is considered the oldest city in the world and the lowest on earth (820 feet, or 250 m below sea level). It has a desert climate, but abundant water sources give it the character of an oasis, and is thus appropriately called "the city of palm trees" (Deuteronomy 34:3). Its first signs of habitation date back to approximately 9000 B.C. Jericho enters written history as the first town west of the Jordan River conquered by Joshua and the Israelites approaching from the east. It was a border city between Ephraim and Benjamin (Joshua 16:7 and 18:12). Ehud killed Eglon here. Jericho is also mentioned in the Elijah and Elisha narratives (2 Kings 2). The remains of Old Testament Jericho are found at **Tell es Sultan**. New Testament Jericho, whose remains are spread out over a large oasis about 1.5 miles (2.5 km) to the south, is probably where Jesus passed through on his way to Jerusalem. It was here that Jesus healed the blind (Matthew 20:29; Mark 10:46; Luke 18:35) and met Zacchaeus (Luke 19:1). Jericho is also mentioned in the parable of the Good Samaritan (Luke 10:30).

A panoramic view of Jericho, the oldest city on earth.

Along the Dead Sea

The **Dead Sea**, an inland lake in the southern Jordan Valley, is the lowest point on earth, 1,305 feet (398 m) below sea level. It is known in the Bible as the Salt Sea, Sea of the Arabah, the Eastern Sea, or simply "the Sea," to distinguish it from the Great Sea, i.e., the Mediterranean. The lake is about 50 miles (80 km) long, 10.5 miles (17 km) wide at its widest point, and reaches a maximum depth of 1,310 feet (400 m). Its extremely saline waters do not enable any marine life but it is rich in minerals. A number of sulfur springs lines its shores and it has become a haven for people worldwide who seek its medicinal qualities. Ezekiel (47:8 – 10) envisions that a river from Jerusalem will enter the sea and make its waters fresh.

KHIRBET QUMRAN

Seclusion in the wilderness after baptism was a common occurrence during the time of Jesus, as evidenced by our knowledge of the Dead Sea Sect, e.g., the Essenes, whose center was at Khirbet Qumran, on the northwestern coast of the Dead Sea. The famous **Dead Sea Scrolls** were discovered accidentally by two Bedouin shepherds in a cave nearby. The Essene sect, who settled here in the second century B.C., functioned as an ascetic cooperative community, rejected established Temple rituals and, among other activities, engaged in writing and copying holy manuscripts. Some experts consider the Essenes to be the forerunners of Christianity. During the Jewish revolt against Rome some Essenes joined the insurgents. When the Roman army approached Qumran in the year 68, the inhabitants hid their holy writings in the caves of Nahal Qumran to the west. Some of these writings were discovered in 1947 and have been named the Dead Sea Scrolls. Coins show the place was again inhabited between 132 and 135 by Bar Kokhba's fighters, before being deserted forever. The ruined settlement was excavated and restored and one can now see remains of a tower, interconnected buildings, an assembly hall, scriptorium, refectory, water reservoirs, ritual baths, storerooms, and a pottery workshop.

(above) The Qumran caves, where the Dead Sea Scrolls were discovered.

(right) The palace-fortress of Masada, looking southeast.

(left) Salt formations along the Dead Sea.

(below) The En Gedi oasis.

EN GEDI

En Gedi is among the most beautiful oases in the Middle East. Meaning "fountain of the kid," it is where the Shulamite watered her flocks and King Solomon sought her among the cascades of water, banana groves, rosebeds and vineyards. David hid from Saul in the "strongholds of En-gedi" (1 Samuel 23:29). At the top of the waterfall here is a stalactite cave, the legendary site of their famous encounter (ibid. 24:1 – 17). The ancient site, west of modern Kibbutz En Gedi, has been excavated and is part of a nature reserve.

MASADA

Masada is about 10.5 miles (17 km) south of En Gedi and a mile (2 km) from the western shore of the Dead Sea. It is the site of the most dramatic and symbolic act in Jewish history, where zealots chose mass suicide rather than submit to Roman capture. King Herod built a fortress complex on top of the 1,310-foot (400-m) high cliff, making it one of the strongest fortresses in Judea. A cable car provides access to the top where there are extensive remains, including the wall, its towers and gates, the triple-tiered northern palace, other palaces, bathhouse, living quarters, storerooms, synagogue, and a water storage system. Surrounding the mountain are remains of eight Roman camps, an assault ramp on the west and remains of two parallel aqueducts in the northwest.

East of the Jordan

GADARA

About 5 miles (8 km) from Hammath Gader (see above), on the other side of the Yarmuk River, in Jordan, is **Umm Qeis**, the ancient site of **Gadara**, one of the ten cities of the Decapolis. The city's territory probably extended not only to the hot springs of Hammath Gader but to the Sea of Galilee itself, since coins found at the site indicate interest in shipping. Like Gergesa (Kursi), Gadara is associated with the miracle of the Gadarene swine. The archaeological remains include a Roman theater, a colonnaded street with shops *(above)*, and baths. A small museum at the site houses a white marble statue of a headless goddess, as well as coin finds. The site offers a panoramic view of the surroundings.

PELLA

Traveling eastward from Beth Shean into Jordan, across the Sheikh Hussein Bridge, one soon reaches the ancient site of **Pella**, one of the cities of the Decapolis. In antiquity Pella was one of the most desirable sites in the Jordan Valley for habitation because of its abundant waters and mild winters. Josephus relates that Pella was destroyed by Alexander Jannaeus in 83/2 B.C. Pompey took over its control in 63 B.C. According to Eusebius, early Christians fled to Pella following the Roman siege of Jerusalem in A.D. 70. Pella remained an important Christian center until it fell under Arab domination in 635. It then slowly declined until finally destroyed by a massive earthquake in 747. Many of the visible remains date to the Roman and Byzantine periods. They include an odeum, baths, several churches (one of which is shown *below*), and a civic complex.

JABBOK RIVER

Proceeding down the valley, about halfway between the Sea of Galilee and the Dead Sea, one crosses **Wadi Zarqa**, the biblical stream **Jabbok** *(right)*, where Jacob wrestled with the angel (Genesis 32:22). Throughout biblical times various sections of its approximately 60-mile (100 km) course served as the western boundary of Ammon, the boundary between the kingdoms of Sihon and Og, and a division in the territory of Gilead.

JERASH

Jerash, identified with the Greek city of **Gerasa**, is about 21 miles (34 km) north of Amman. Its ruins are among the most well preserved in the region. The name appears in the Bible only in its adjective form, where the territory is described as the country of the Gerasenes (Mark 5:1; Luke 8:26), where Jesus miraculously healed two men possessed by demons (see above, Kursi). Tradition has it that Gerasa was founded by Alexander the Great. A city of the Decapolis and of the Roman Province of Arabia, Gerasa prospered until the third century A.D. when a shift in trade routes caused its decline. The extensive remains include temples to Artemis and Zeus, an elliptical plaza (forum) with an impressive colonnade *(below)*, a hippodrome for horse and chariot races, two theaters, a triumphal arch commemorating a personal visit by the emperor Hadrian, baths, and churches. At the Southern Gate is the Visitors Center, where entrance tickets to the site are sold.

AMMAN

Amman, the capital of Jordan, is the biblical Rabbah of the Ammonites (Deuteronomy 3:11) and the Roman Philadelphia. Inhabited in prehistoric times and again before 1500 B.C., the city became a fortified settlement early in its history. David besieged the city and captured it. It remained under Israelite control throughout the period of the United Monarchy, but regained its independence shortly after the Israelite division. Rabbah was destroyed during the Babylonian conquest (590–580 B.C.). Rabbah, rebuilt and renamed Philadelphia by Ptolemy II Philadelphus (285–246 B.C.), became one of the cities of the Decapolis and an important commercial center. The ancient Citadel on the summit of Jebel el Qala contains the sparse remnants of a Roman temple to Hercules, a Byzantine church and an Umayyad castle. Next to the Citadel is the Jordan Archaeological Museum, a small building with an impressive collection, including a prehistoric skull from Jericho and some of the Dead Sea Scrolls. The second-century Roman theater is set into the slope of a hill near the downtown area. Inside it is the Folklore Museum. The ruins of the odeum, a smaller theater from the same period, are nearby.

MOUNT NEBO

South of Amman, and some 5 miles (7 km) northwest of Madaba, is **Mount Nebo**, from where Moses gazed upon the Promised Land he was not permitted to enter. "And Moses went up from the plains of Moab to Mount Nebo, to the top of Pisgah, which is opposite Jericho" (Deuteronomy 34:1). From here one has a spectacular view of the Dead Sea and Jordan Valley. On the summit of one of its twin peaks, Siyagha, are remains of a Byzantine monastic complex that served to mark the site of Moses' burial. The ruins of biblical Nebo are on the adjacent mountaintop of el-Mukhayyat.

(above) Modern Amman, with the Roman theater in the foreground.

(left) Looking out from Mount Nebo towards the "Promised Land."

MADABA

Madaba, originally a Moabite town, rose to prominence in the Byzantine era from which its many mosaics date. The most famous of these constitutes the only ancient map of the Holy Land in existence, decorating the floor of the Greek Orthodox Church of St. George. At the center of the colorful map is Jerusalem and the Church of the Holy Sepulcher. About a quarter of the mosaic remains, dating from the time of Justinian in the mid-sixth century.

The Madaba Map, showing the Dead Sea, Jordan River, and the walled city of Jerusalem, 6th century.

MACHAERUS

Machaerus, dubbed the Masada of Transjordan, was Herod's southernmost stronghold east of the Dead Sea, about 14 miles (22 km) southwest of Madaba. Built by the Hasmonean king Alexander Jannaeus (103–76 B.C.), it was one of the strongest fortresses in Judea and served as a base for Alexander and Aristobulus in their resistance against the Romans. Herod's wife escaped from Machaerus to her father, Aretas, in the Arnon Valley, about 12 miles (20 km) to the south, when Herod tried to replace her with Herodias. Herod subsequently occupied Machaerus with Herodias and Salome, and here John the Baptist died (Matthew 14:3ff). In the Great Revolt, Jewish zealots were starved out of Machaerus by the Romans and the fort was razed.

A general view of Machaerus.

The Rift Valley and the River Jordan

A satellite picture of the Holy Land.

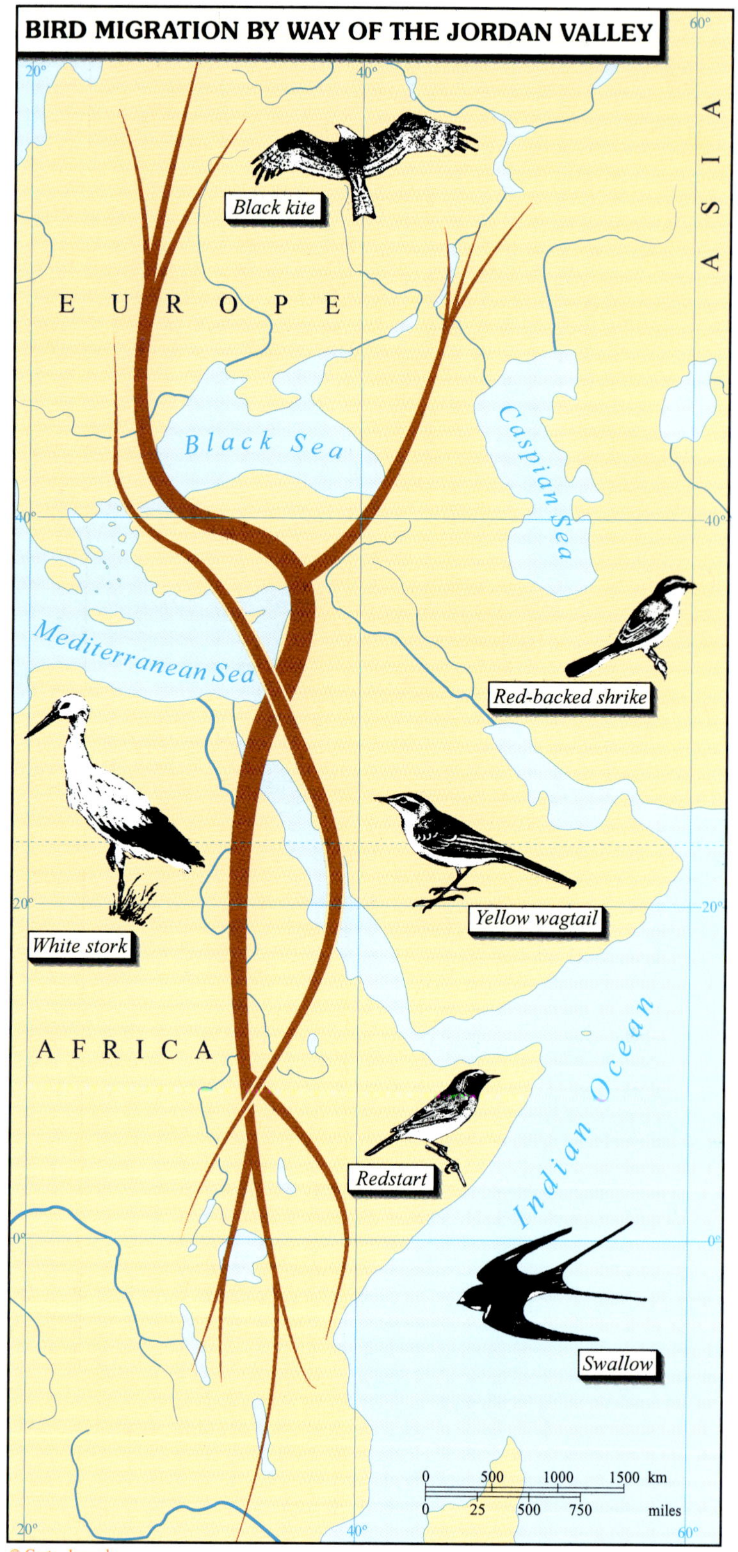

The Jordan Valley, and the Arava to its south, are part of the Syro-African Rift. Originating in Syria in the north, it runs for about 4,000 miles (6,400 km) to Mozambique, Africa, in the south. This valley is noted for its unique landforms, distinct flora, and saline hills and lakes. One major feature, the lowest place on earth, is the Dead Sea, variously called the Salt Sea, Sea of the Arabah, and Lacus Asphaltites.

Because of Israel's unique geographical position—between the Mediterranean coast in the west and the Syro-African Rift in the east—the skies of Israel serve as one of the major migratory routes for birds flying from the northern hemisphere to Africa and back again.

In the autumn season, birds pass through Israel's coastal plain on their way to the warm regions in Africa and in the spring, they return to their nesting sites by way of the Syro-African Rift. Thanks to this phenomenon, of millions of birds of numerous and varied species in its skies, Israel has become a world center of bird research and observation, causing thousands of scholars and enthusiasts to come for this fascinating spectacle.